D1091352

Walking the Boundaries

By the same author

Walking
the
Boundaries

Poems
1957–1974

Peter Davison

Secker & Warburg · London

This selection first published
in England 1974 by
Martin Secker & Warburg Limited
14 Carlisle Street, London W1V 6NN

Designed by Philip Mann

436 12550 1 (hardcover)
436 12551 X (paperback)

Printed in Great Britain by
Cox & Wyman Limited
London, Fakenham and Reading

For Angus and Lesley

Acknowledgements

The new poems in this volume originally appeared,
sometimes in rather different form or with different titles,
in the following periodicals, to which grateful acknowledgement
is due:

Antaeus (**Doors**), *Antioch Review* (**At the Close, Call Sign Aquarius,
Poem of Force, Bandages**), *The Atlantic* (**Standing Fast, Ground,
Into the Future, Walking the Boundaries: West by
the Road, The Obituary Writer**), *Counter/Measures* (**Embraces**),
New American Review (**The Heroine**), *The New Republic* (**Bed Time**),
The New Yorker (**The Dance of the Hours**), *Ploughshares*
(**Asking Nothing, Valentines**), *Poetry* (**Walking the
Boundaries: North by the Creek**).

Dark Houses was originally published in 1971 in a limited-
edition booklet by Halty-Ferguson Publishers, Cambridge,
Massachusetts.

Contents

8

Peripheral Vision

The corner of the eye
Is where my visions lie.
A startle, or a slant
From squirrel, bird or plant,
Turns hard and fast if seen
By eyes asquint and keen.

Rather the shape and style
That only just beguile
The tail-end of my sight
Than organizing light
To tidy up the view
And clear it out of true.

North Shore

(for Charles Hopkinson)

1 The Embarkation for Cytherea

The sun is high. Young Saxons shouldering oars
Trample the shaven lawn. Platoons of girls
In organdied profusion follow them,
Flowers of Boston's bright virginity,
Cool limbs beneath frail garments. At the pier,
Piled high with picnic baskets, cutters ride
The hospitable swell, their halyards eased
Yet eager to spread sail. Across the strait
The islands rise like rain-clouds from the sea.
Here on our hill the house, after its crowded morning,
Will sleep till dusk. Then we expect them home,
Their wine all drunk, their faces gorged with sun,
Guiding their ships with briny headsails furled,
To quiet moorings.

2 The Return

                    Many years have passed.
The house and I still wait for their return.
Shutters keep out the sun, chairs lie in shrouds,
The Chinese vases rattle with dry leaves.
Angry with age, but waiting, I keep watch
High in the eastern wing, my spyglass cocked
To sight the flicker of those homeward sails.
Perhaps they are all dead? I have not heard
A youthful voice for years. When will they come?
The sea still glimmers, empty of islands now.
The lawns are empty. Over the weathered house
Gulls hover, wailing their disdainful cry.
At night the house is silent, and the wind
Steals out each dawn to comb a barren sea.

Summer School

These tenants of the migratory season
Were children yesterday. Adulterers today,
They settle like thievish cuckoos in such nests
As they can find furnished with a summer vacancy,
And share their sandalled quest of the absolute.

Professor P., expert in semantics,
Teases their drowsy mornings with a lecture;
But once the sun announces afternoon
They strip naked in each laboratory sublet
Among worn counterpanes and last winter's books
To dedicate each fiber of themselves
To the hot discipline of appetite.

Thus in the academy of summer
These scholars, sworn to seek the limits of self,
Enlarge their own by feeding upon others
And learn by process of elimination.
What bones will they have gnawed when they return
To the major business of the autumn
With knitted brows, to read once more of love?

The Peeper

No sound—yet my room fills up with thunder.
Behind their windows ladies dance for me,
Heedlessly languid, moist, sumptuous,
Naked as newts. Oh with what zest
Have I applauded wifely treachery,
Lovers in closets, husbands unsuspecting,
Greedy embraces once the door has shut!
Lit by electric light, flesh in a window-frame
Gives pleasure keener than clasping lovers know,
And I make no objection if the shade
Snuffs out the final postures of the act.
Night is my library; day deafens me.
I cringe to hear girls gossip, clatter round corners,
Scold shabby neighbors, squeal at the bus to stop.
Flesh under glass strikes no such dissonance,
Nor troubles touch nor smell nor taste. Hands off!
     I love at eyes' length!

To a Mad Friend

I may look fine at the moment, but like you
I have capered and somersaulted in the street,
While, hoisted upon my shoulders, someone's face
Smiled at my friends and answered the telephone;
Or hovered, like a fish with nose against
A rock, in elements I could not breathe.
You've seen us in every land you've travelled through:
Our ties were tied, our shoes were always shined,
But icy eyes and tightness around the smile
Are marks enough to know your brothers by.
Rest easier, friend: we've all walked through your dreams
And are no strangers to that company.

The Suicide

Poor starling. Her cry was sharp enough to draw blood
As she braced her whistling head and squeezed her feet
Clamp upon her local chimney top
And glared as hard as the sky that looked her down.
Taut-muscled on the ground, she pecked and pecked
Whatever she scratched up, and never sure
Which grains were food, which grains were only gravel.
Just so her loves, random as a vine.
Curse those who kept her food from her until
She'd learnt their tricks! Her hungry eyes became
Their sentinels, on watch for where the heart
Lurked, to have it out and peck peck peck—
And yet her beak most often fell on bone
Until the day she turned it on herself
And dizzyingly sang, within her throat
The sigh of the slain, the grunt of the executioner.

Artemis

See how this girl, trim,
Fragile as porcelain,
Poises within herself,
Standing apart with hounds.

Chaste in her garments, loins
Crisp as a boy's, her knees
Rigid as spear-shafts,
She stares down a victim,

Lowers her eyelids,
Lets the white linen fall,
Stretches, as unaware
Of the blood rising,

Curls like a kitten,
Unclenches her fingers,
While her demented eyes
Flutter in hiding.

Now, when the hunt is closed
Hard on the quarry,
Savage in chase at last,
'Die!' she screams, riding.

Sacrificial Mask

Mirror, Mirror on the wall,
Who is falsest of us all?

Only silence. Does this mask
Hear no questions mirrors ask?

I have modelled every crease
To ensure the people's peace

Who go easy when they see
Kindly love encasing me.

Now the eyes behind the face
Blink their horror and disgrace.

They know well what price was paid
For the features I have made.

Hunger

Western gods are seldom fat:
Priests and painters see to that.
Christian men at grips with Mammon
Show their fealty by their famine.

Smiling Buddhas of the East,
Plump and padded from the feast,
Pensive, wonderful and wise,
Feed the hollow Buddhist's eyes.

Hungering Buddhist solves the test
If he sets his mind at rest
By the Way that Buddha set him:
'You, who love your god, forget him.'

Yet, in matters Eucharistic,
Westerner is proved the mystic:
Though the mystery defeats him,
If he loves his God, he eats Him.

Spells in Sawyer's Cove

That was no dream. The shapes
That bared their grinders
And flapped their pinions
Will not be kept inside
The boundaries of sleep.
They must be exorcized
Or lived on even terms with.

Do you recall occasions
When, mid-morning, your feet
Were seized upon by rhythm
You never remembered hearing?
How hard it was to shake off?
How, for a night or two,
Your dreams played you an endless
Game of what, when a child,
You played as Fox and Geese—
But with magic at the center
Now, no placid patch of ice?

These paths must be retraced
(Remember?) foot by foot
In rhythm like peristalsis,
As powerful as sun,
The heartbeat of a worship
For centuries forgotten.
Forget? If you forget
Sever the thread that stitches
You to your senses. Here
On islands, among forests,
Tree-darkened, fog-enshrouded,
The dances of your shambling
Ancestors recover
The sources of their being.
The demons and gargoyles
That grimace in your sleep
Are lurking in that forest.
You cannot cast them down.
Now in fog-throttled silence
An idol carved with flint
Out of soapstone crouches central
Summoning you to approach
With offerings of flowers.
'O god of seas and forests
Give virtue to our dances.'

Finale: Presto

'I think I'm going to die,' I tried to say.
My husband, standing over the bed, labored
To hear words in the sounds as they emerged.
He shook his head as briskly as a dog
Taking its first steps on land, and acted deaf
To the words he knew he might have heard me speak.
Throughout this evil month I've said the same
To every visitor. It comes out gibberish.
The night nurse, hiding in my room to smoke,

My daughter, prattling anxiously of clothes,
My son, weary from four hundred miles
Of travel every weekend—all escape
By smiling, talking, plumping up my pillows.
I wrack myself to utter any word;
They reply, 'Dear, I cannot understand you.'
If I could move this hand, this leg, I'd write
Or stamp a fury on the sterile floor.
I'd act the eagle. I, who winced at death
If the neighbor's second cousin passed at ninety,
Who bore an ounce of pain so awkwardly
It might have been a ton, who fed myself
With visions of good order in a future
Near enough to reach for—I am cumbered
With armlessness, with leglessness, with silence.
To say the word so anyone could hear it!
Death, do you hear me, death? The room is empty.
Only the one word now, hearers or no.
I batter at it with convulsive shouts
That resonate like lead. Again. And now—
Listen—it rings out like a miracle.
No one stands near. The corridor is dark.
'Death.' I sing the lovely word again,
And footsteps start to chatter down the hall
Towards my bed. Smiling at every sound,
I see that no one can arrive in time,
And I, emptying like water from a jug,
Will be poured out before a hand can right me.
That word raised echoes of a halleluia.
Death, do you hear me singing in your key?

Not Forgotten
In Memory of N.W.D.

1 **Watching Her Go**

Drawn by her mumbled entreaties,
We gathered wordlessly around her bed.
She lolled there, shrunken, grizzled,

Garlanded in feeding-tubes, damp with sweat,
Plucking, when she remembered,
At the dressings from the last operation.
Look! Could she have stirred at the touch
Of my hand? Or was it another wave breaking?
The eyes opened. Pain burst at me
As from a cannon's muzzle.
They closed. Flaccid, fumbling
At the unravelled edge of herself,
She died like an otter sliding into a pond.

2 Dream

I stood alone at a funeral. It was up to me
To pronounce the oration. My tongue was knotted fast,
And every mourner rolled his maggot eyes.
The reek of greenhouse flowers pressed on ears
Still filled with Handel's 'Largo', while the bright box
Gleamed like a conference table, proof against speeches.
Towards the rear of the chapel, twisting kleenex,
Sat ranks of visitors, urged to stop in on their way
To another appointment by friends who had assured them
This would not take long. It was taking longer and longer.

Who was dead? It was up to me to remember.
I had ransacked my pockets twice—no memoranda—
And my Oxford Book of Consolations had vanished.
The penguin crowd creaked folding chairs impatiently,
So with nothing at all to say, I did what I did:
Danced a very respectful dance on the coffin.
The guest of honor drummed her cold toes
On the underside of the lid.

3 Reality

Have I no right to howl—not even now
When the cradle has been empty and cold for years,
The feeding-bottles broken, the rocking-horse rusted,
The christening-spoon bequeathed to hungrier mouths?
Her friends owned her as well: she had nursed so many.

They came together at last, a crowd collected
To watch the last flutter of a fountain, and turned away
As workmen tramped in to pry up the ancient stones.
But they turn away with a sigh: they cannot howl
Simply because they are not frightened enough.
They have lost a landmark, not a birthplace.

4 Self-Defense

I came to hold her hand
And sit beside her bed.
Her body was lightly manned:
The siege was in her head.

She counted rags of rage
And wore them while her breath
Grew shallow stage by stage;
Yet persevered in wrath

Against the runaway
Who roused a million cells
To take to their dying day
The habits of cannibals.

Her courage conquered me.
When she asked an end
I yearned to grant her plea,
To serve her like a friend.

Now I can weep no more.
My pain is almost mute.
I did not lock the door.
I did not execute.

5   Aftermath

The world now has
A gray look to it.
There is much less strangeness
Left in strangers.

Mountains have shrunk,
Trees loom with less shadow,
Even the flavor of fear
Tastes as diluted.

Yet the bloom of your presence
Is absurd as unicorns
Or buttercups at Christmas.
Just as your girlishness
Glanced out daily
From within thickened
Middle-aged flesh,
So does memory
Find you hovering
In a hundred places
Or standing
At the center of the music.

I pray you, do not stray
Farther from us.

Jenny

Jenny takes water seriously,
Strokes its ebb and burrows its rush,
Explores the grotto's twilight hush
Under the silence of the sea.
Jenny takes water seriously.

Jenny hovers on whistling air
In westerlies that laugh aloud.
Balancing upon a cloud
Or wringing sunlight from her hair,
Jenny hovers on the air.

Jenny listens while the earth
Shifts its mountains, nurses grain.
Groping with roots beneath the rain,
Sleeplessly alert for birth,
Jenny listens to the earth.

The flickering fire in Jenny's blood
Every morning brighter burns
With flames like crisp uncurling ferns.
Let desire's midsummer flood
Free the fire in Jenny's blood.

The Star Watcher

(*for R.F.*)

Stars had the look of dogs to him sometimes,
Sometimes of bears and more than once of flowers,
But stars were never strange to him because
Of where they stood. We knew him jealous
And in his younger days a little sly
About his place among the poesies;
Yet when his eyes showed envy or delight
They rested upon knowledge, not on distance.
All that he saw, up close or farther off,
Was capable of being understood,
Though not by him perhaps. He had enough
Of science in him to be optimistic,
Enough of tragedy to know the worst,
Enough of wit to keep on listening,
Or watching, when it came to stars. He knew,
Across the distance that their light might travel,
That nothing matters to the stars but matter,
Yet that their watchers have to learn the difference
Between the facts of knowledge and of love,
Or of love's opposite, which might be hate.
Therefore he taught, and, like the best of teachers,
Often annoyed the students at his feet,

Whether they learned too much or not enough,
Whether or not they understood him wrong.
Two was his pleasure, and the balance held
In love, in conversation, or in verse.
With knuckles like burled hemlock roots, his hands
Had, in his age, smooth palms as white as milk;
And, through the massy cloudbanks of his brows,
His eyes burned shrewdly as emerging stars.

Death Song

The summer day is kind. A breeze
Surrounds me, as if tenderness
Were its invention. Set at ease
With all my selves, I smile and bless
    These friends: the leathern sage, the mild
    And unambitious aging man,
    The rebel boy, the gifted child.

I bring no trophies from the past
And wish for none. The Deathless Four
I was when young have merged at last.
Time was I wanted nothing more.
    Reduced to one, a single breath,
    The weather breathes me in and out
    Till I shall join with it in death.

Bordered by forest palisade
Whose stiffened hemlocks creak and groan,
A clearing keeps me in its shade
Until I come into my own.
    The waxwing grass has just the hue
    Of glossy hair I loved the most.
    That truth, at least, was not untrue.

I gave away what self I had
To love and loyalty. No doubt
What use they made of it was mad,
But could not self be done without?
    The breezes curry me as though
    Their mind turned on a single breath
    To keep me or to let me go.

The sky is higher now. The sun
Has dwindled to a coin of gold.
I cannot hear the river run.
The forest shade has lost its cold.
    The weather takes my breath away.
    This is the place prepared for me
    Where, without menace or decay,
    The earth will set my body free.

from **The Breaking of the Day**
(*Genesis 32: 24–30*)

July

The afternoon is dark and not with rain.
Intent on conquest, the sun presses its attack
Harder as the blunt day closes in.
Swallows like knives carve at the thickening air.

I swab the sweat from my blistering hide and walk
Burnt, unblessed, my brain inert as alum.
I stagger beneath the weight of the day
Like a three-legged dog howling curses at the climate

Until, defeated by the weather's bludgeon,
I lift my hands to half a god
And stammer out a portion of a prayer.

The Gift of Tongues
God my father spoke in the calm of evening.
He spoke in iambs beating in the darkness.
His pipe glowed and its vapor blossomed upward.
The child at his feet drank in the heady honey
Of his voice, his presence, his attention
While the elm-leaves rustled their assent.
The words he spoke—from Oreb or from Sinai—
Were, had I known it, many times outworn
Except for those that burned as his alone:

> *I shall come back to die*
> *From a far place at last,*
> *After my life's carouse*
> *In the old bed to lie*
> *Remembering the past*
> *In this dark house.*

His voice wore all the costumes of our tongue,
And in the dark I trembled at the golden
Din of the past resounding in my ears.
These were the words that God had always spoken,
As, 'This is my beloved Son, in whom
I am well pleased.' The words belonged to him,
And now, as their custodian, he gave
His hoard to me at night beneath the trees.
I counted them for years before I learned
The spending of them; yet I did not know
That he had given them away for good
And that from that night forward he would walk
The earth like any natural man,
His powers incomplete, his magic gone.

Delphi
The crackle of parched grass bent by wind
Is the only music in the grove
Except the gush of the Pierian Spring.
Eagles are often seen, but through a glass
Their naked necks declare them to be vultures.

The place is sacred with a sanctity
Now faded, like a kerchief washed too often.
There lies the crevice where the priestesses
Hid in the crypt and drugged themselves and spoke
Until in later years the ruling powers
Bribed them to prophesy what was desired.
Till then the Greeks took pride in hopelessness
And, though they sometimes wrestled with their gods,
They never won a blessing or a name
But only knowledge.

        I shall never know myself
Enough to know what things I half believe
And, half believing, only half deny.

Life Mask

The self inscribes itself upon the face
With signs that age alone cannot complete
Before the mask has settled into place.

Appetite, sorrow, labor, all compete
For every pore of skin and ridge of meat.
The self inscribes itself upon the face.

Beauty fell back, already in retreat
Before the heart sat steady in its seat,
Before the mask could settle into place.

My face, a stranger in the mirror's neat
And family frame, had many friends to greet.
The self inscribes itself upon the face.

Deface, defy, distract, corrupt, or cheat,
Whatever the name, the face will show defeat
Before the mask has settled into place.

My paces not yet learned, I set my pace.
By forty, someone said, the tale's complete.
The self inscribes itself upon the face
Before the mask can settle into place.

Rites of Passage: 1946

Through a window the wind
Went leafing through my book
A chapter at a time.
A fearsome way to spend
Those Saturdays in June—
Stealing my hundredth look
Past the ice cream saloon
While studious prose and rhyme
Stood sentry to my crime.
The summer dusk inex-
Orably drew me where
The tyrants of my sex
Should stand and smoke and stare,
Shuffling outsize feet
At the corner of our street.
This summer was the first
That brought me to that town.
Our house was tense and small.
Those boys were large and brown.
No matter what the thirst
That drove me to the shop
Where they had gathered first,
I trembled lest their call
Might summon me to stop.
They whistled at the skirts
And laughed with hideous
Suggestion at a blush,
Still louder at a glance,
And felt their khaki pants.
They combed their oily mat

Of hair. They yawned and spat.
Their names I had not learned,
But others of like size
Had bullied me at school,
Connived with me in lies,
Had hurled and batted balls
With brilliance and surprise
And trained me in the rule
Of locker rooms and halls
Where victory was earned
And secret passion burned.
What was there to know?
The thunder that we heard,
That turned us limp and pale,
Our clumsy bones absurd,
Our fingers aching from
The need to touch and tell
The belly's muscled swell
That one was not enough
To sample smooth and rough,
To hold heat in the palm—
Ah, what was there to know?
Inveigling with a hand
At night, by day we spoke
In arrogance and brags,
In excrement and leer
And hunted down the weak
Like poisoned contraband.
The weak were always fags.
The strong were never queer.
Give me another smoke.
Look at these knockers here!
The girls we left behind
Lived in another age,
Walked gracefully as foam,
Looked down, were soft and still,
Giggled when put out
For lack of fist or shout.

They could not have been real.
No wrestling? No rage?
No laughter? Who can win
When there are only smiles?

Here in a strange town
I stand before a book
In a climate swollen with men
Who scuffle and leer outside
Across a street I cannot
Cross, a lifetime wide.
For nearly twenty years
I shall not turn again
To hang around with the boys,
To lean and take a look,
To whistle at my fears.
I shall burrow among women.

Song

Past the rich meadowland of the senses
Shade mingles and stirs in the clearings.
In that island where oranges blossom
    I seek you, child, again.

On the shore where surf scurries hissing
And the sand scrapes under your shoulder,
Where tides nuzzle sweetly together,
    I hold you, child, again.

In the heat of wet tongues and embraces,
In the shuddering bed where Love
Can never quite be requited,
    I lie with you again.

That childhood has lasted forever
In a forest of tottering archways.
Sink down in the echoing moonlight
    And die with me again.

The Collector

How the meadows dazzle this morning!
Every songbird's throat is gasping
To swallow deeper draughts of sunlight.
The fresh flowers gape as thirsty as the birds.

Like the web of a net my path crisscrosses
The piebald fields from wood to marsh
On the trail of plump lady slipper
Or openhearted blackeyed susan.

They flee me—lupine, arbutus, arethusa,
Dawn flowers fresh as the birds' dawn song—
Yet I am patient. There will be others.
Journeys end in lovers meeting.

Another day, another conquest:
The blush in the shadows, the crisp stem,
The velvet flesh against my fingers,
Head drooped prettily against my chest.

Hardly a field without its encounter!
Here are my prizes; here again, flowers
Taken in unlikely places and postures.
Some time I could tell you stories.

As the years pass, I take greater pleasure
In boasting where I found heart's-ease,
Forget-me-not, all the pretty creatures
That yearned so ardently from their dewy beds.

Eurydice in Darkness

Here far underground I can hear the trees
Still moving overhead where he, the poet,
Mourns. Let him stir stumps if he chooses.
Soon enough he'll sing his courage up
To penetrate the earth, clinging to that lyre
As though the world depended on it, and unstring
One after the other of my familiars,
(The three-headed lapdog, the boatman at the river,
The gaggle of furies, my Undertaker himself)
With instrument still twangling from the effort.
His fingers will be raw, but I'll be waiting
Dressed to kill and ready with a plan
He'll find acceptable. He'll turn his back
(Its every flabby muscle I have pinched
A thousand times) and clump along the tunnel,
Dead certain I shall follow him to sunlight.
And so I shall—murmuring at times,
Whining that he walks too fast, complaining
That he might at least give me a look
After such absence, brushing my breasts against him.
Not till the sunlight seeps in overhead
Will I tax him: a man and not a poet
Would have kept the country free of snakes
And left off that everlasting mooning and fiddling.
He could have prevented all this! And he might, please,
Give me a hand here, I'll fall with these sandals.
That's it! He turns from the light, his face engorged
With pity and self-pity. He thrusts out his hand,
And I shall dance away, my laughter dancing
Before me every mile of the way back home.

Dance of the Shaking Sheets

Once we have discovered
How the heart grows old,
Leaving us no house
Against the cold,
We huddle for survival
And enlace
Body into body,
Face to face.

Hungry for compliance
That we once possessed
In the days of lap,
The days of breast,
We curl in the nest
Where we lately lay,
Savoring its softness
One more day.

There we know no hunger.
Surely more alive
Than when awake,
We shall survive
Stuttering rifles,
Deaf to the spit
Of angry bullets.
Let them hit.

Muffled under cover
We can bear
Any victim dying
Anywhere.
Rocking in the cradle
Of a lover's thighs
Softens the hunger
In her eyes.

Danger cannot penetrate
This womb.
Body, give us shelter.
Banish doom
Distant as the rifles
In the war
We refuse to study
Any more.

Having Saints

God has become too vast to pray to
for anything in particular. Not so saints.
Saints have at least a mouth to be remembered.
They did not build the world. They carried
only their own burdens. God is beyond us,
inhumanized by the long passage of time
since anybody saw Him. Even His mother
has stiffened over the centuries, until
the Church, recently, promoted her into heaven.
Saints have their presences on earth, thank God.
They carry keys or swords, they visit prisons
or in unhappy times have their breasts torn off
by pincers, even as you and I.
We're not ashamed to tell our small desires
to Paul or John or Nicholas or Teresa
in hope they needn't be passed on through channels.
We may even confess to them our grudges and panics.
A saint can be bargained with, done honor to
in exchange for favors granted, can be asked
to set his kindly parasol between
the searing sun and my poor eggshell head.
Prayers and pleading lie not so far apart
to give all praise to God, no plea for myself.
No god worth worshipping would listen to
a prayer that had no sources in desire;

but One who spins the galaxies is not
an Ear to whisper into. Lord, give us saints
even if we elect them for ourselves.

Gifts

When I was a child, a heartstruck neighbor died
On her birthday. Dying was strange enough,
But what a way to choose to spend your birthday,
I thought, and what sort of a gift was this?
From time to time, people have done it since—
Dying in the environs of a celebration
As though they had picked out the day themselves.
Perhaps they had, one way or another,
Prayed for something to happen, and prayed wrong.
Sophocles, when old enough to die,
Suspected prayer and entered a caveat:
'Zeus, act kindly whether or not I pray;
And, though I plead for it, turn harm away.'
I keep a wary silence on my birthdays,
Make up no lists at Christmas, lie low
When asked what I *really* want. How should I know?
Best ask for gifts as though I had none coming.

The Immigrant's Apology

You think me citified, love?
Hard-shelled, headstrong,
Undoing all errors
With deftly trained fingers?

I am forced to step shrewdly
Through these byways perilous.
From every casement lewdly
Leans a crowd of faces of girls.

I am an islander, love,
Trained in taboos (Never touch
Hate with your left hand!),
Nourished on little and much,

Bred to believe
That ghosts guide bodies.
City ghosts do not bleed
With this our blood.

The journey here was long,
The boat, small,
Contrary winds, strong.
The sight of the towers was fearful.

Over the black pavement
Insect natives carry
Skeletons outside their flesh;
They click, they scurry.

My bones, love, lie in hiding.

Lunch at the Coq d'Or

The place is called the Golden Cock. Napkins
Stand up like trumpets under every chin.
Each noon at table tycoons crow
And flap their wings around each other's shoulders.
Crumbling bread, I sip at the edge of whisky
Waiting for my man to embody himself
Until in time he shadows the head waiter
And plumps his bottom in the other chair.
Once he is seated with his alibis
We order drinks, we talk. His voice is rich.
Letters I had written him all winter
Had washed my mind of him, till Purdy,
Warm of heart and hearty of handshake,

Had shrunk into a signature, a stamp.
The fine print vanishes. I see him plain.
I know my man. Purdy's a hard-nosed man.
Another round for us. It's good to work
With such a man. 'Purdy,' I hear myself,
'It's good to work with you.' I raise
My arm, feathery in the dim light, and extend
Until the end of it brushes his padded shoulder.
'Purdy, how are you? How you doodle do?'

For Amphibians

I say my goodbyes
To orange peels, eggshells,
Chicken guts, celery,
Row a stroke homeward,
Then wait for gulls
To pick the stuff over.
Gulls are getting choosier
Here in the tideway,
But the sea never stops
Gulping and nibbling.

Bottles, bravest
Of all the garbage
I scuttle offshore,
End up mumbled
Down among the lobsters.
Tides or a loop of line
Sometimes unwater them:
What was clear, clouded,
Messages faded,
Contents doubtful.

Landsmen like me
Are shocked when sailors
Turn to the sea
As the place to retire

Whatever's unwanted
From soup to cadavers;
Yet they draw on its water
For all but libation
And bite without fear
Into fish that have eaten
Whatever we feed them.

The sun sinks down,
Crossed by a cormorant
Hastening homeward.
I turn to the oars
And row myself out of it,
Make my skiff fast,
Stamp feet on shore,
My pail rinsed clean
Of provisions, garbage,
Salt water, all.

To walk the path landward
I turn my back seaward.

Letter from a City Dweller

Only from islands can you shape the city,
Plumes bobbing from a hundred miles away.
Towers like tusks jut out from the horizon.
It makes a handsome profile, from a distance.

Invisible of course from islands are
The cells and walk-ups that we use for hiding,
Nor can you hear the language of the streets.
The city has would-be islands of its own:

Neighborhoods—the few that still remain—
Cliques and clubs, gangs and offices,
All the niches where an anyone
Can lose himself and find himself at once.

Such camouflage is hard to achieve on islands.
Your trouble is that there you always know
Exactly where you are. The sea and land
Leave you no ambiguities on that score.

Islands provide no place to hide
From him or her or them or from yourself.
They offer you exposure to the sky
And silence, to the wind and stinging rain,

Even to fellow-men. While you can watch
The city from a distance, our shivering city
Has set so many walls up for protection
That islands are less visible than ever,

And fewer islanders stay home to vote
Every election. Not so our citizens,
Who multiply like pages being printed
Without a binding or conclusion.

Yet even though we lead a sheltered life
We have advantages unknown to you:
We pick and choose: we never meet the poor
And can with ease ignore their poor existence.

We have built barricades against the cold
Of weather and of hearts: for we believe
That there is really such a thing as comfort,
That it can be possessed as well as given.

Islands offer aspirants a chance
To learn what can be learned from nakedness,
Since there clothes serve exclusively for weather
And not as one more form of hiding place.

The danger on your islands is that you
Can grow so giddy as to think the sea
Will always be content to be your servant
And that your selves, astride their tiny kingdom,

Can shake their fists at all that lies onshore.
Sainthood is perfect training for an island,
As islands are for sainthood. So it was
With John, enraged in his cave on Patmos.

He beat his breast until the walls resounded,
And answered in his Book. At intervals
He peered from the cave's mouth, downhill to the harbor,
Where shipping came and moored, unmoored and went.

Angry each time, he turned back to the cave
Where the Great Beast crouched, hideous and waiting.
Such enterprise is suited to an island
If that's the work you like. I wish you luck.

But keep in mind, winter is cold offshore.
We're glad to see you when you're passing through.
When you haven't caught sight of a smile in ages,
Don't hesitate. Take passage for the city.

Travelling Among Islands
(*for A.R.*)

Alone, alone but not without resources
Even in his melancholy smile,
He keeps as property no more than a razor
And a laundered shirt to take him through tomorrow.
Clean as a cat he sits, nibbling his fingers
To make himself still cleaner, tooth and nail.

Love he knows in plenty—all the love
A sailor finds in port, with every girl flowery—
But he loves them dearly as they wave goodbye,
And all his friendships are perfect in chance meetings.
Departing, he leaves others to remember
And moves toward another destination
Where faces will wash clean again to see him.

Only the sea is home to him.
He is nourished by land as others are by water.
He lives on less than would supply a lifeboat
And his lovers lie in wait among the islands—
Circe, Penelope, Nausicaa, Calypso.

The Emigration: Newfoundland 1965

Love, there are reasons why I must be free
        To put to sea.
     No matter how the body aches
To keep in touch, touch has its failures too.
The mind is helped to heal by travelling,
       And so I offer to the wake's
         Brutal unravelling
The old perplexities of course and crew.

My dream has never changed: abandoned far
       From shore I float
     Aboard an ill-found boat
Unhelped by oar or sail, landfall or star
To guide by. Currents jostle me at will.
      The wallowing shallop makes her way
        Through the long day.
I cannot steer; I must not let her fill.

Halfway between the city and the island I
      Am bound for the city.
     The island had its terrifying
Pastures. There the bones of strangers lie
Unburied where we slew them without pity.
      We watched them, dead and dying,
        In the long light
And hugged the memory for many a night.

In flight from the unspeakable, we float
      Our household in a boat,
    Leaving behind us every grave
Of every ancestor we can recall.
The family mountains fade over our stern.
     The children, large and small,
      Whom we must save,
Turn their eyes forward to the land to learn.

Those children's hopes are here aboard with me,
      Adrift, adream, at sea,
    The peaks of home receding,
Alert for land across the wrinkled moat
Of ocean, without confidence or pity,
     While the strangely guided boat,
      Nobody heeding,
Moves its unknowing cargo toward the city.

Love, though I left you, smile on my return
      From the ancestral shrine
    Where blood will not again be spilled.
I would not travel now except to learn
More than the city teaches about sin:
     First, that that blood must be fulfilled;
      Second, that it is mine;
Third, that the island cannot take me in.

    Halfway between the city and the island I
      Am bound for the city.

Easter Island: The Statues Speak

We are asleep, at peace. The grass has woven
A blanket for the fallen few who lie
Dreaming supine, watching the trade-wind clouds
Glide overhead. Our uplands are deserted.
Safe in settlements along the sea,
Shepherds avoid the hillsides we inhabit.

Now come newcomers, bringing means to force us
To rear up again, hillbound on rocky haunches,
Pitilessly to search the sea-surface
And guard the grassblades in their little seasons.
Aboard new rafts that snuffle past the reef
They make for landings on our lava beaches
To set about their plan for resurrection.
They hope by disinterring us to save
Themselves from meeting themselves at the fatal crossroads.

Our feet stood fathoms underground. Thin soil
Clothed us to our chins. How we hoped
To be forgotten! Now these new arrivals,
Who place unearthly burdens on God, unearth us.
They prop us upright for the hundredth time.
They will gladly let us sleep again
Once they have learned the reasons for our silence.

Castaway

Out at sea, out of sight
of city or island, where waves
lap like tiles on a roof
reared over earth, there eyes
see nothing to see, there ears,
wave-wasted, have nothing to hear.
Only the sea of the blood
that sings forever behind
the ear and the eye, that recites
the syllables of spirit, now
makes itself heard or seen.
Old ocean parches the hide,
withers hands and fingers
and invites the drying flippers
to spread like fans, the fins
to gather into a tail,
and, smooth as a seal, the trunk

without so much as a whisper
to thrum its way to the bottom.
Only if heels, horniest
and hoofiest end of the body,
can keep their longing for land
may the mariner preserve
his true landworthiness;
kick them up, dig them in,
remembering earth to the last
where, alone, water has meaning.
Earth is always most
itself at the edge of the sea
where, rising at last from the salt,
Odysseus clambered the rocks
and, drinking deep of the spring,
his muscles wracked and torn,
shielded his salt hide
with a fresh green branch, and lay
beneath its shade to sleep.

Calypso

She found him facing out into the fog
At the edge of the sea, stooping, winnowing
Stones with all the care of the demented,
Hurling them into the murk, low along
The surface, skipping them like petrels.
He wandered by the shore, halting and stooping,
Leaning abruptly for additional
Hates to send spinning out to sea.
She watched from the cliff over his restlessness
And ached to hold him in her arms—held
Herself away from him, for an embrace
Would only remind his body of its bruises.
Hobbling a step, stooping, sorting the stones,
Hurling them again, as though he hoped
To force them, slippery beneath the sea,

To draw him after them, he threw and threw.
The shore wind whipped the bracken by the path,
Pressed out against the fog which yielded to it
And took it in and closed and gave no ground.
A woman could do nothing for him now,
Though she had known for months that this was coming—
Long before he guessed, even before
She herself could have put it into words—
His occupation gone, his enterprise swallowed.
The tide was out, the stones lay high and dry.
Terns chirruped in the fog along the shore.
The fog pressed on the land a little closer
And she could scarcely see him now, while he
Would never look back to where she stood behind him,
Just as he would never know that she
Had watched him strive, delude himself, and fail,
Had known all his evasions and deceits,
His minor infidelities, his hopes
That this time shabbiness would go unnoticed.
The only way to show her love for him
Was learning how to stand unseen
Until he chose to notice her—to laugh
Or storm or touch her breast or ask for food
And, though she was invisible, to smile for her.
Now in the fog he'd wandered farther off
Than she had ever lost him, yet she still
Was more aware of him and his despair
Than fog and sea and wind and stones together.
And so she turned, knowing herself helpless,
Leaving her man to men's devices, and the wind
Struck at her face as she walked weeping home.

After Being Away

When I shall die, in body
or mind, if you survive me,
give me my due. You know

I held no certain magic
and threw no light before me.
Searching out of pain
at first, then out of habit,
and out of self at last,
I stumbled on surprises
and managed to record them.
There's only one surprise—
to be alive—and that
may be forgotten daily
if daily not remembered.
Sometimes I remembered it.

You too, my love, have watched
each day for its surprises
and touched them as they happened.
Forgive me for inflicting
my pride on your surprises
and holding to the few
that were my sole possession.

Surprise we had together
in afternoon or evening
when we were close together
or even, often, parted.
I thank you for the thousand
surprises that you gave me,
not least the gift, unhinted
and endlessly surprising,
of never being absent.

The Two of You

I

Your face is tense as wire within a wire
    When you consent to bed with sunlight flying.
The dervish flashes up into the fire.
    Not to be lost to love is to be dying.

Molten and greedy, quivering in my arms,
    You gnaw, you tear, you moan beneath my prying.
Our veins are full of sunlight as a field.
    Not to be lost to love is to be dying.

These fearful bodies rage against our will.
    (Our love is truth and leaves no room for lying.)
These stones, these walls, this house, this windowsill
    Are not to be lost. To love is to be dying.

II

Outdoors the breeze blows childlike, notwithstanding
    Tomorrow it could be carrying sounds of war.
As we pass, we turn toward each other
    Like lovers in a bed.

We preserve house-plants, growing creatures,
    By constancy of warmth. In their season
Light airs are given entrance. We exclude only
    The brazen winds that turn flesh into stone.

Nourished by our senses and attentions
    This house will open up into a palace
Where children dress themselves in royal robes
    And swagger with the certainty of angels.

To hear one another's voices without speaking
    Composes the music of this house. The time
Of storms is welcomed as a penance.
    This house is silent and fragile as God.

Brotherly Love

My first and milktooth madam,
You walk in every woman,
Tinting her with the haze
And fever of the nursery.

I cracked you in my arms
Before I knew their uses
And sucked the brine of sex
At the blue moons of your bruises.

Outmaneuvered by wave
On wave of skirmishers,
You bear my scars as keepsakes
From foot to forelock.

At the far end of the row
My mind has hung your portrait.
It sees you thin and thirsty,
Then plump and pink and suckling,

Responsive as a mistress—
Whilst, unobserved, the certain
Secret hands of the hangman
Prepare themselves for business.

The Last Word

When I saw your head bow, I knew I had beaten you.
You shed no tears—not near me—but held your neck
Bare for the blow I had been too frightened
Ever to deliver, even in words. And now,
In spite of me, plummeting it came.
Frozen we both waited for its fall.

Most of what you gave me I have forgotten
With my mind but taken into my body,
But this I remember well: the bones of your neck
And the strain in my shoulders as I heaved up that huge
Double blade and snapped my wrists to swing
The handle down and hear the axe's edge
Nick through your flesh and creak into the block.

Old Photograph

Eight years dead, and dying
Many months before that, you leave me
No trace of yourself, except
These yellowing prints and some letters.
What do we know of the dead?
The needle of memory scratches
In the effort to remember.

Everything has been taken care of,
The papers are filed,
Most of the photographs mislaid
In a cigar-box.
Only this propped-up pose remains,
Rigid on the mantel in pious memory.

While you were dying I shuddered
At every jolt of pain that shot through you,
Watched as you speechlessly
Contorted with a numb tongue
To speak of your dying.
I was told I would forget that
And retain the memory of you
In the sounds of your husky laughter,
Your charm in company,
The glee you took in never
Saying goodbye on the telephone.

It isn't true. 'True feeling
Leaves no memory,' as Stendhal said.
It has left me nothing of you
But reminders that remind me of nothing.
Besides, only grief, sleeplessness,
Infant despair, betrayal.

These are you. I know nothing else
About you any more. I live behind glass,
Framed as tightly as your picture,
As frozen, as rigid, as blind.
How can I keep in touch
When there is nothing to touch?

23 September 1967

Afterwards

Sit down with me and rest,
    Beloved guest.
These gardens I have made
    Where summer shade
Is shaken from leaf to leaf.

Here is no desert where
    Death circles in the air.
Here the rich scent of fruit
    Has clambered from the root
To triumph on the bough.

Behind us lies the earth
    That tricked you into birth
And troubled you to death.
    Deny its names for grief
And anger now.

No longer flinch and stain
    To have it out with pain
Nor stretch your will to break
    What blood cannot forsake.
Now I have paid your debt.

I do not call you here
>   To close your eyes with fear,
Despair, or counterfeit.
>   Recline beneath the shade
Of gardens I have made.

Words for My Father

If God chooses you to have a son, tremble:
For just twelve years you may remain his father.
From twelve to twenty, try to be his teacher.
Thereafter you may hope to die his friend.
>   A Mexican villager

1   Voice
Your gorgeous voice soared
down the flumes
of the tumbling canyons.
Sentences and judgments rang out
with the clarity of air that knows little rain.
Giver, trainer of tongues,
even cottonwoods do not grow without water.
Your voice's notes were poetry, pity, war.
It restored bodies to the dead.
It taunted my mother, turning you into her child.
It sharpened the duellers' blades of long-forgotten rages.
It yearned for the doting and the pity of your children.

2   Voyage
I came to the sea after twenty years
and sailed to inquire
through all the trafficked harbors of the world
for news of my father's victories.
The voyage brought home little but pain,
messages garbled in transmission.
The air was dry and silent.
My father's eyes turned away
from the knowledge-swollen face of his son.

3 Dead

Later, when death began paying
its visits,
we were manacled by the knowledge
of how my mother, infuriatingly patient,
had bound us together.
On the voyages since, another ten years,
we have kept silence like Greeks
'carrying heavy urns full of the ashes of our ancestors'.
More men and women have died.
We have not forgotten
your mother's rectitude, her shabby flirtatious plumage,
nor your father, whose testament
was leaner than you desired—as every father's is.
His blood has scalded you
but you need not share his blame.
Give him your blessing.

4 Road

I walk forward in the afternoon of dying
along the road of words, cruel to the feet.
The dry tawny hills below your orchard
stretch away without shade or the sound of water.
Not yet in sight of you, I hear your
cough, your parched and grating throat.
Shall I answer the question you are sure to ask?
If you are Odysseus, my son, come back,
Give me some proof, a sign to make me sure.
I have three signs: the scar, the trees, the words.
The scar of our parting, which has never healed.
The trees you planted, felled, buried under rubble.
The love we shared, carried by words only.
Deeds overwhelmed us.

5 Words

Words need not always fail.
Now matter how seldom
we gather ourselves

to gather our hopes
into flocks, herding them before us
to huddle in their pens,
they are our dearest gift from this sparse soil,
the locked and grudging earth. They are
our servants, our sacrifice, our pledges.

Your gift to me
is my gift to you.

Pretending to be Asleep

If a man could pass through Paradise in a dream, and have a
flower presented to him as a pledge that his soul had really been
there, and if he found that flower in his hand when he awoke—
Ay!—and what then?

Coleridge: *Anima Poetae*

I The Deserted Poet

This part of the country is underpeopled.
Not a word waits in hiding under the ferns
To reach up for my hand and lead me out
Of myself. No words have passed this way this season:
I have forgotten even the sound of their footsteps
Whickering through the leaves at my approach.

Look at my face, never an honest one.
It covers my desertion by pretending
That words have never meant a thing to me.
This face settles for the lie. It puts on
Creases of feigned anger between the eyes,
Furrows of mock surprise across the brow.

I wear the mask of an actor who returns
From a long journey to find his wife and children dead.

II In the Dock

Tried by the day, I stand condemned at night.
The evidence of years of fraud and shame
Waits until darkness to be brought to light.
Crime hangs from every letter of my name.

Each day conceals its treachery and blight
In places no defendant could disclaim:
Beneath the shirt, the mattress, out of sight
Behind the portrait smiling from its frame.

Night comes to sentence me. My second sight
Fixes me steadily within its aim
And squeezes slowly. With a shriek of fright
I fall forever from the cliffs of blame.

Watching my body vanish, I awake
To hear the sounds I never thought to make.

III Under Protection

One side wet and one side dry,
My skin walls out the world.
I am blockaded, only barely in touch.
Life stiffens and keeps its distance.

I coast in tides of light and cold
Past knife-edge noises and the smoke of cities.
The daily lives that shoulder the sound of my name
Seethe distantly across the flats of time.

I have dreamed myself into the streets
Of a village on market day. Aloft on the battlements
I command the town, and prepare to seize
The contraband bartered by the peddlers.

Boots dazzling, muscles like halyards,
My subordinates stand tiptoe in their barrack,
Braced at unblinking armed attention
For the clang of the summons to suppress disorder.

Out there the life could be just anyone's,
But it happens to be mine.
And do I govern it, pay taxes on it?
No, it is mine, but it offers me no friendship.
It surrounds me.

IV The Flower of Sleep
When danger strips the mind
And slithers toward my throat,
I slink away in hopes to stay
Alive, aloft, afloat.

I cringe from the land of light
To bury myself in sleep
As though a sea surrounded me
Of endless dark and deep.

There dreamers hand me flowers,
Presuming me to be dead.
'No reason why he'd choose to lie
Asleep in a death-bed.'

In this cradle of desperate rest
I snore away all fear—
The toppling tree, the storm at sea,
The Goddess striding near.

Such sleep does more than dream,
For when the sounds of day
Bring life to sight, I welcome light
To shudder my fear away.

But lately I dream of sleep,
Of wrecks and falling trees,
Of flowers laced around my waist
And grappling at my knees.

V   The Public Garden

1

This public park and I are strangers.
Look at it; sit on its benches; no matter.
It sleeps though I am agog in its presence.

2

My turn to sleep. The park enters my privacy.
It wakes trembling in the spaces of my skull.
Its dry bones burst, its benches are my lovers.

3

Each day the avenues I roam at night
Shut down when I awake, and no pretense
Of sleep will penetrate their spaces.
The visiting hours are over in the garden.

VI   The Visitant

You make yourself known to me in surprising places:
A laundry or a bus, or late at my office desk
After the others have gone, or where I listen
To an unspoiled voice read out a familiar poem.

Distracted, clouded over, I am startled
Awake by your presence stealing up behind me
To draw my breath and raise your hands and clasp
The soft familiar palms over my eyes.

VII   Pretending to be Awake

I am disgusted by the earthworks of my protection.
The clothes stink that curtain my nakedness
And beneath the wool my flesh is beginning to fester.
I must tease my life awake that now lies sleeping.

Others stay awake in the dark by laceration,
By thrashing out at workers, lovers, children,
To keep their ears alert to the sound of sorrow.

Some plunge into the tolerance of women
Or paralyze the tendrils of their brains
Desiring visions beyond sleep or waking.

If I could tempt this sleeping life awake!
It shuns me now that sometime did me seek.

VIII　The Cost of Pretending
I would despise myself if I had the strength for it,
Would welcome the knife slitting the skin of my neck
As long as it did not falter and pour the blood.
Give me your hand, put it beneath my arm
Which closes on it, next to my heart. What
Do you hear of me? A steady beat, dull, leaden,
Irreversible. One who survives everything
Will shortly survive even himself.

IX　The Voices
I know those voices. They are all mine.
Tuesday the infant,
Wednesday the child,
Thursday the grown man wheedling
In rut or yearning in prayer,
Friday the sexless ancient, dreaming of sex.

Through the country of sleep
The voice of my blood
Trickles like water over limestone ledges.
Tributaries borrow its *bel canto*
To stage-whisper their way through dreams
Or heroize the arias of nightmare.

The voice is me, whatever voice or stream,
The voice of history rising through my sources.

X　First Voice: The Child
Strange feet upon the stairs
Turn and walk this way.
I clothe myself in sleep

By shutting off my light.
They will not find the scent
Of hate on me tonight.

With one huge sigh, my chest
Moves easy, at the rate
Of every thief who breathes
More slowly than his guilt.
The door creaks open, but
My face, disguised in sleep,
Sings children's choruses.

The door has shut. The steps
Give way, descend the stairs.
The light, the book, emerge
From hiding. Like a bear
In blankets, all alert
For footsteps to ascend,
I lurk here in my lair.
They come? Then I'll pretend
Again to be asleep.

XI Second Voice: The Youth
What wakened me? Moon?
Rustle of willows?
A cry or creaking stair?
Or was it shadows
Troubling my sleep
With a tug at my pillows?

Out of the shadows
Where sleep had been hiding
An ominous parcel
Comes quietly sliding—
Charred bones and ashes
On the tide riding.

Who could the parent be
Of this delivery?
Hands cold as serpents
Fumble the frippery,
Wrench at the wrapping,
Pause and lie quivering.

No, let it lie there
Inside its adorning.
Now should I stand to arms
After such warning,
Or pace the aisles of night
Until morning?

XII Third Voice: The Widower

The world has spread the word
That I am unworthy of it,
Crouching in lairs and caves
Pretending to be asleep.

First of the warnings: Love
Opened her eyes to me,
Then stopped her breath. No more
Pretending to be asleep.

Next came attentions, lavished
By divorcees and widows.
Though I took their bodies, mine
Pretended to be asleep.

Then came the nights, each darker
Than the one before. By night
I had no part to play.
By day I seemed asleep.

I know the sun by name.
This darkness may give ground
If I dream my way awake,
Pretending to be asleep.

XIII Fourth Voice: The Grandmother
I am an old woman living in a house beset with men.
It has been years since I heard a child
singing to itself.

These little men of mine are so little mine.
They live in the same dwelling but at a terrible distance.
They bring me their flowers but never notice me.
They wrestle with themselves,
with each other, father and son,
at all hours. I carry them platters of food.
They eat. They think themselves to be alone.
They walk like crustaceans.

There is no way for me to say, 'Awake.'
I must go on forever, smiling, serving, alert
for the accident of their waking.

Once young men stirred out of sleep
and smiled to find me naked beside them.
They gave me the flower of themselves,
the flower of their dream.
My little men do not yet know
they have been presented flowers.
They cannot recognize the face of the beloved
in their dream. How can they know,
unless they wake, that they have only
been pretending to be asleep?

XIV Possession
Inside me lives someone who writes poems,
Someone who has no words but from time to time
Borrows my words, whirls them through the dance
Of his purposes, then returns them.

My only evidence for his existence
Comes when I find poems on my desk
Ready for me to revise.
                    When did this happen?

Though I have never known who scribbled them
In secret, still I know my job.
I find them ready and waiting, I take over.
Possession they say is nine points in the poem.

Making Marks

No two conventions of teeth behave alike.
Some chatter, grip, or slash. Others strike.
Thirty-two counters measure out our breath.
What other course for words but past the teeth?
The human body holds them at its height
Better to speak with, but the worse to bite.

Teeth hold the resonance for speech and song,
Which cannot rise past tunelessness for long
Unless teeth govern them to soar and lilt—
To pierce with love or hate up to the hilt.
Smiling, though soft in cheek, is hard in bone,
And sounds make words by trickling over stone
To give the tongue an edge to call its own.

Sounds are the stuff, yet letters are the knives
In each man's voice, the shape of what survives.
Dry bones alone can live, though fossilized
Forever. Let my words be recognized
As mine by the wear of their bite. They classify
The being that they once were brandished by
And the abrasives they were sharpened with.
This way he gnawed his life and grinned his death.

A Word in Your Ear on Behalf of Indifference

History is sometimes salvaged by it, a civil servant
Who bows and smiles at weakness, at right and wrong;
At progress, poverty, peace and war; at victims,

Torture, and torturers. A skilled masseur,
Indifference smooths our faces into features
And lets our muscles work without rending each other.

Indifference-in-the-home lets tiring lovers
Share a warm bed between the defloration and
The signal for the soon-to-be-contested
Divorce to plunge both parties
In ice-water up to the arse.

Though we yell back and forth, 'Let us erase our existence!'
'Let us scurry before the flailing winds of our senses!'
'Let us surrender into the hands of the forces!'
Indifference chimes in to discourage us from jumping.

My client gives us the power this side of death
To shackle ourselves, to live within our dimensions,
To ignore for hours at a time
The outrage and the dread
Of being no more than we are.

The Pleaders

What are you going to do with us, who have
No edges, no talents, no discriminations,
Who hear no inner voices, who perceive
No visions of the future, no horizons?
We are among you; we are going to stay.

We crush, we drag, we heave, we draw the water
For you to spill. We gather together to listen
To your speeches, though your tongues run on so fast
We cannot follow, and your jokes dart in and out
Too quickly for our laughter to form itself.
We are your children, whom you treat like horses.

When crowds surge out into the streets
You have invited them; we run with them.
You give us order, speak on our behalf,
For we speak up too slowly to interrupt you.
We are the numbers ranked on your computers.
We are among you; we are going to stay.

If we knew how to pray to you, we'd pray
That you could listen long enough to listen
To what it is we think we want. We know
That what you think we want lies far away
From anything that has occurred to us.
We are your children, whom you treat like horses.

We are the eyes your eyes have never met.
We are the voice you will not wait to hear.
We are the part of you you have forgotten,
Or trampled out, or lost and wept to lose.
We are your children, whom you treat like horses.
We are among you; we are going to stay.

What Counts

Our astronomic signallers are sure
That what they send is monitored Out There.
Whether the creatures who receive Earth's signals
Wear flesh or bone or neither, the reply
We get will be conveyed to us in numbers,
So those who man this world must be prepared
For grammar with no language. (A pulse, we call
Such signals? But that stands for blood with us.)

The words we use to amplify our numbers
Will count for little. Though they 'see the stars',
Our far communicants can send us nothing
That we have any names for—only numbers

Which in space-dialogue refer to nothing,
Not food or love, but only to themselves.
It could be heart alone that counts out there,
But without language we shall never know.

1968

For days the television seared our eyes
with images of the many-widowed family.
We crouched to stare at their loosened faces, their fingers
on rosaries, the hunched and harnessed shoulders.
(We starve for what survival has to teach us.)
Term after term their champions had been chosen,
served, shot down, reciting Aeschylus
and Tennyson. ("'Tis not too late to seek
a newer world,' and other familiar quotations.)

Too late, as usual, the latest killing
instructs us in our love for those who seek
more than we think of seeking. Soft in our seats
we watch the people of the long procession
reeling out across the summer landscape
to hide a body shredded and cold with bullets.
No one can hold his tongue: shrilled editorials,
New Year's resolutions, blurted promises
drown out the inner yelp of unmastered hounds
who press and snuffle hungrily along
the course this body leads us. At last, at night,
his remnants vanish in the grainy ground.

Before and after death we coursed that body.
No matter if words attacked, we could shrug them off,
but his image aroused our desire and nudged our hatred.
Slogging up mountains, seized by rapids, breasting
breakers, standing stripped naked by crowds,
his body sexed us. It revealed a self
our mirrors had never included. Gawky, controlled,

athletic in action, hectoring in speech,
it performed deeds that could have broken us
and left us with the trophies of last year's hunting—
whistles, grunts, imitated animals.

'Change,' his body said—but when we heard
our voices speaking, they were not our voices.
His body has emptied the screens of our sight.
The people are not listening to voices.

The Losing Struggle

'Is my thought a memory, not alive?'
                    Wallace Stevens

To yield words easily gives pleasure
To the tongue that speeds their flow,
But, loosed, they linger on the surface
Like unexpected, unpenetrating rain.

Where are we to seek the words for life?
And how are we to see what must be seen
Before shaping our language to the sound of it?
What must be seen is every moment present

But hardly every moment seen. What I hear,
Like the muttering of a crowd, is seldom discerned
Although the murmur is never interrupted.
My body secretes against its rarest need.

When released, by lightning or alarum,
I can run like a deer, ravage like a lion, overhear
The creak of a mouse's toe on a wisp of straw.
Except for these times I sleep.

What are the repositories in myself
That bind me in the caverns of silence
And refuse to let me ramble at my will?
My ego stamps its foot at their refusal.

By the shore the sun embraces me.
The pleasures of water ripple through me
And take me by the singing throat.
The elms across the lake shine out like torches.

By another shore I watch the ocean scurry
Over its deeps of flounder and periwinkles,
Bearing its rockweed aloft like torches.
As its tide falls and the sandbar emerges, birds alight.

Here by the sea I cannot see as far as the mountains,
Nor do they loom over my shoulder as they once did.
Change is everything here, here everything changes,
Changes with the phases of the moon.

I have come to worship the sun, clouds, clarity,
And as deeply I distrust the moon.
I cannot bear the monthly flow of blood.
Tide and change corrupt the imagination.

I spin my fancies finer and finer,
A quota of gossamer every working day
From an old spider who does not care for flies
And webs it for the sake of the design.

My name is death. I freeze the world in light.
I see my arm, poised at my side to move,
But never moving; and my eye, my eye
Is fixed on what exists beyond existence.

Stumps

The field is studded with their thousand lives.
All that is left of all that tracery
Pokes through the goldenrod in amputations
Too short to see, too tall to be mown over.
Their knuckles sprout new fingers every April.
I go my rounds in August trimming them back.

The roots, now elderly, are just as far
Involved in growing as they ever were,
But their suckers are sickly and cannot survive
Unless they're given help by God or me.

After a year or two of this flirtation
I snap trees off by hand which saw and axe
Once needed all their edges to bring down.
Poison could lull these lives to a merciful end,
But I as owner claim the dark indulgence
Of giving them a chance to sprout once more.
Crops like mine are not so much planted as buried.

Walking the Boundaries:
West by the Road

Now swift swallows have flown for the winter.
The last pears have fallen.
Maples, huddled close in the swamp,
slip off their leaves
and lay bare the shaggy cliffwall.
Twigs in damp tangles under
the sagging grasses
abandon themselves to rot,
food for beetles.
Hardiest of their generation, wry apples
clutch at gnarled branchlets
as long as the wind will let them.

The sumac's crimson seedpods cringe
while the air unleashes the first
fast rangers of milkweed.
Under the deep beeches
in leafmold crevices
autumn phalluses
rise up in a single night from
forgotten woodpiles.

The screech of a bluejay batters
naked oak trunks, scattering
bleached goldfinches
wherever they cluster on thistles.
The junco's tail flashes
in the cedar. He sings
of two pebbles chipping against one another.

Toppling grasses and unsteady leaves
tolerate the chickadee's scramble
through the drowsy apertures of autumn
toward the house
whose chimney sighs grey woodsmoke
and panes of glass smile earlier each evening.
Roots hunch and contract, their blood runs thin.
They hold forearms
stiff against the wind, while
castaway stones
plunge fistlike for winter
into the ground's gravelled belly.

Sighing, chuckling, the minnow-busy
creek's summer-warm tides,
heartbeat of the sea,
steam and scurry.
The thatch of the marsh holds hard:
it crouches down on matted fibers
to quake at air but yield its seed to water.
Come January, grumbling glaciers
will walk uphill in the arms
of northeast gales to shear
a year's marsh hay
and macerate against the granite
piers of the bridge
the buried shells of snails.

Moles burrow down to the frostline.
Starlings hang on in holes
hard-won from woodpeckers.

Squirrels, walled up between
skyscrapers of hickory nuts (all
stolen except for a handful
of windfalls wrapped in their husks)
duck down under the barn.

Snow is coming. Snow
is coming. All but birds
will be buried. Water will
absent itself till spring,
while earth locks up into its mineral meaning.
Only yesterday we breathed a world
of liquor and seed. It hardens now.
The little animals lie panting,
sleepless, winterless,
anticipating drift and flake,
awaiting the crackle of frozen meat
upon the tongue. Their lungs
bloom like flowers
at the alienation of the air.

Is Anything Wrong?

(*for Margaret Atwood*)

I do not know what I mean. Perhaps you know.
These lilypads, these ghostly gingkos and herons
stretch up their presences from the anti-world.
I live and move among visions; I hold
my being in my hands and cannot recognize it.
What sort of creature am I inside of?
Pressing closer to the knowledge
that there is no knowledge, that our world
is visions, shadows, I hear it rumored
that perhaps, who knows, we are living in a cave?

Doors

I know what lies behind them in the attic.
I have been filling its dusty corners for years.
Those pigskin suitcases, with ancient labels
from Karlsbad or København, no longer fit
even for storing woollens, have been covering
for the wrong man.
Toys with a leg broken,
cartons of dead letters, not one of these
means a thing now except as part of me.

I am bursting, dying.
My body is broken.
The rooms might be as empty without me
as they are already empty of the dead;
and I am even emptier than the rooms
for I contain them.
I am not a plant, I am dying.
There is no bud-time for me, no seed-time.
I am a chieftain without a tribe,
a lover without a bed.
My arms fly at my sides, my knuckles pop.

A woman is listening to me.
She leans forward, she sets her hand on my knee.
Her eyes shine.
She listens, she understands.
I cannot do it without her.
Pascal said the greatest fear in life
is the fear of sitting quietly in a room alone.

I peer up the stairs. I strike a note.
There is no one there to see, to hear,
under the rafters. The loneliness
in this last room is infinite.

I have shut my past in here
behind the doors I have closed,
and all the rooms contain me.

The Heroine

She was one of the few I can speak of who believed
in personal destiny; the only one who swore
by holy writ that death was worth gambling on;
the meanest spirit to claim a martyrdom
since sainthood ended. What a cunning braggart
she was, a frailty who pictured herself
as a rider of skis, of waves, of men, of horses.
She lugged about a pessary in her purse
like a baloney sandwich in a lunchbox
and referred to Dylan Thomas and Dostoevski
in the tone of voice reserved for former lovers.
Breck hair, white scarves, clean flesh, hard muscles,
sun-worship, and a trough of molten and remorseless work.

I've seen her love-letters—those she wrote
to other men while she was using me—
and her hate-letters—those she wrote
to me while she was using them—but only once
or twice her tiny writing in a different hand,
tilted across the page, wounded but credible
as the early morning trail of half an earthworm,
speaking of her selfhood in the tiny voice
that had been hers as a child, hers once as a girl, hers, hers.
In the usual rooms she spoke in a voice more humble
than the one she wrote in, cozening her larynx
to belie the costumes of ambition, clothes
Mother had dressed her in to go to school.
In saddle shoes and pageboy bob, disguised
as Betty Boop, inculcable, unresisting,
she set out bait for poets and professors.
She was as innocuous as Lenin in Switzerland.

The acrid sun tugs at her shrinking skin.
Out in the desert, blankeyed from deceptions,
she hugs herself to herself, learns how to ride,
to hate, to write, to broadcast, to give milk.
Her husband and her children, grating on her,
teach her a little more of how humans do it,
of how humanity must learn to sleep.
But then the tiny voice within her voice
struck up its canticle of loathing for
ambition's wigs and masks. Off with disguises!
Snarling and sobbing like an orchestra,
she levelled the forests of ego,
whirling around her bare blonde head
a sword as holy as a samurai's.

London 1972: Silent Zone

How this city has altered! The newly erected
Dark Tower surpasses other towers,
pricking its searchlight into
every bedroom. Housing
coats the ground like stickum.
The borders of the express roads
glimmer and flicker all night.

Did the lovers (real or imagined)
who fondled my hands in these very streets
never smile? Of course the traffic
could not have boiled along
so thick. We're locked within
a Silent Zone. We can be fined
for blowing horns at one another's ears.

Did we really, true loves or not,
never never smile? Did not the parks, packed
with benches, deck-chairs, bird-life,
throng in the fifties as they do this Thursday?

Who has begotten all these portly children
and dressed them in costumes bristling like armor?
The streets of my city were wet with rain.
They summoned with murmurs,
with love hung out like wash from every window.

Those tender-fingered lovers are sick now,
strayed, splayed, or dead.
I am not the he I thought I lived with,
dancing at the end of someone else's
string. Self-guided now,
I can make out no welcomes on the faces,
no women in the windows,
no children on the islands.

Asking Nothing

The words carry themselves as carefully
as a muscular woman tricked out in sequins
walking a high wire.
I ask nothing of them, I only
set them in motion as gently as feathers.
Birds exert themselves more than the words do.
Hunger compels them, they cannot choose but fly.
Words, who seek no food for themselves,
follow a leader they have not chosen
in an order they have hit upon without deciding.
Only those words are admitted that speak of their speaker.
Whether they speak well or ill of me
is not their business nor even mine.
Their only need is, they should speak a language.
Having walked a way, they return to silence
leaving only the memory of the drum-roll,
the sequins, the spotlight, the high wire.

Poem of Force

Sacrifices meant nothing to *me*.
I loved every inch of him: his wrestler's muscles,
his tanks and his missiles naked as mine.
How I kissed his statesman fingers
and his soldier toes!
I tattooed on his breast
the imprint of my body.
Even while sleeping or drunk I guarded
chest, notch and boundary against his skirmishes.
Never have I understood an ally so well.
He is my darling wolverine.
Keeping him fed full with nourishing rations,
I surmount him like a tower, and he smiles
in gratitude as I draw black blood
from the bodies of his children.

Embraces

1 The First Stranger
She wants his way! He's won! His will, set free,
canters inside his head, and fingers grip;
she nestles close, suggests with tooth and lip
the time is past for play;
her hands, the bolder pair, direct his way;
he is astonished at such avidness,
shrugs out onto the plain of nakedness
to find her there, an offering; he nears
what cannot be reversed; he summons in
his wits to guide his memory and smears
bookish caresses on her stranger skin
until her breath reminds him: it is She.

2 New Stranger

Awakening to strangeness, standing
first, then sitting (knees too weak
for standing) side by wakened side,
they smirk with stiffened faces, hear
the flesh that cries out in its sleep.
The floor tilts them together, forces
them to keep a stage's width between them
and stalk out of the crowded room like actors.
They sit with every follicle
alert while they permit a car
to carry them somewhere. At last
the engine coughs and dies.
A tree topples. That first touch looses
a cataract which outlasts the moon.

If I saw you now, again,
what words would our bodies know?
How should a tongue remember how
it counted all your syllables
over and over while the moon rose smiling?

3 Same Old Stranger

Puffed like a silken sleeve, your body
dimples under my sausage fingers
as we give over to double dreaming,
slithering over each other in silence
(except for the sound of separate gasping)
to give it to each other here, this body
I call mine grappling the one you call yours,
wrapped in summer sheets, wet
with sweat and (soon to be) with semen,
giving it, giving it, giving it
to the humped and whimpering stranger
who soon will lie beside me, knowing only
I too am wet, I too am awake.

4 Family Reunion

Dreaming of scattering mists I awake
to the warmth of a breathing and browsing.
My hand is touched. A shoulder tingles.
A breast is tapestried over with hair.
No dream, no dream.
Our bed puts by the fragrance of sleep
and takes on the liquor and odor of waking.
The hand rambles. I swim out of myself
into the lake of your flesh.
Fractiousness and humdrum spatter
of chattels and children
of meals and mercy
go shying away.
Our bones go begging, breathing like bells.
We rise through the plaster ceiling
majestic as two full moons,
till, far off, tenderly as a heron circling,
unaware that a footfall has been chosen,
we drift back through the bivouacs of darkness
breathing easy.
We alight on the earth,
enter the house,
sigh deep down into the dens of our bodies.

The Obituary Writer

*There are two voices, and the first voice says, 'Write!' And the
second voice says, 'For whom?' . . . And the first voice says,
'For the dead whom thou didst love.'*

> John Berryman, 1968, quoting Kierkegaard,
> who in turn is quoting Hamann.

When I reach out towards the body of happiness,
a hoarse voice warns me off: 'No no. Not *you*.'
It must be the obituary writer,
the one who scrambled into print the hour
each poet died, always the first to know.
When off obits. he spoke for Henry, defendant.

Then he waved goodbye, and jumped from a high bridge
and clattered dead on the ice of the Mississippi.
I felt him falling all the way to Rome
where I took up pen and paper, an obituary
writer's obituary writer. I got as far in time
as Mayakovsky. Soon enough death spoke,
shouting in a hoarse voice. My pen fell. Outside,
across Largo Febo, barely out of eyeshot,
an old mad woman had unmouthed her teeth
to save them for another life. In bib and blanket,
with stockings swathing her ankles, she set her body
adrift from the fourth-floor windowsill. She encountered
the January pavement with a cry.
Soon the *polizia* were snapping photographs.
Neighbors huddled together in knots, muttering,
their faces gray as hers. We all mooned over
the swollen object laid out on the cobbles.
The skull was crushed. The flung hands had turned purple.
No one knew her name, least of all the papers.

Dead Henry, better known to all the papers,
was noted alive because, sober, he suffered the shakes;
drunk, he shrieked and ranted. Who could stand
to stay in the room with him? Not prissy me,
who couldn't abide the hoo-ha, the abasement,
nor my own flinching from his open pain.
His head was full of everybody's death.
His pants sagged, his fly gaped, his hullaballoos
of falling-down drunkenness were an insult to the brain
no matter how hotly and crisply he employed
hangover time for his mettlesome minstrel show
of dreams, obituaries, exhalations.

Some obituary this is: not that of a friend
nor even of an accountant for the fact
of death, of bodies falling alive from heights
in January and landing dead. Admit
that poetry is one of the dangerous trades.

No matter how many we know who have been goaded
by its black promises to deliver
their bodies to the blue snowdrift of death,
it was not poetry, but life, they died of.
Since the day the old woman took her teeth out
and John the master minstrel turned away
from the gravel of his brother Henry's voice,
there has been no avoiding this obituary.

Into the Future

Standing here just short of the corner
I grope with fingertips
against the rasping surface of brick.
If it had handholds I would hang on.
One move could ruin everything.
They would find my blood running down the wall.

In times like these
one never retraces steps. Forward
is the only direction. Beyond this corner
the wind gusts cold, coughing wave-
whirls of dust along Michigan Avenue.
If I let go and turn the corner
what will come at me from my blind side?
A newspaper clutches my leg and forces me on.

Bandages

As I lie still
here before the sun's
stealthy invasion
of my bedroom window

birds deftly insert
their spring songs
and strip off my sleep
like bandages.

My skin is cold.
Unwilling to stir
either finger or toe
of my whiteness,

I lie unmoving.
Today is the same. Once more,
last night,
no healing.

At the Close

We limp along the shoreline
scuffling and probing for shellfish
alert enough to eat. Each time
stupefaction chokes us, we stare for breath
out across the sea, abloom
with a jungle of algae.

Birds and hot-breathing beasts are few.
Reptiles have the best of it,
preying on the tumbled bodies
of gulls, on fish that breach
the tangled surface of the sea.
After dark, thallophytes
whisper the truth.

Nights are warmer than formerly.
Everything takes forever—
writing, walking, even stooping,
most of all sleeping.

(I cannot snooze for an hour
without dreaming of drowning.)
At greasy daybreak our faces flush
and we are giddy and quarrelsome.

Still, we have more to marvel at
than ever, especially sunsets.
The earth hangs on to air
enough only to breathe—none
to make love, none to make war.
The planet hisses with oxygen.

Walking the Boundaries:
South by the Wall

The trees are choiring their light at the house.
A new-minted copper beech stands burnished
at its greening sister's side
crying aloud with the zeal of its leaves,
which have unfolded today like lemurs'
fingers. In the swamp ferns uncurl
their bedsprings. The meadow grass,
as thick as fur, crowds on itself
to gobble up yesterday's rain.

No passageway is left in the pasture
for large-footed beasts, only room for speckled
clutches of eggs and the tender claws
of new-hatched fawn-spotted pheasant,
hiding and scuttling between the scented
trunks of grass-stalk and grass-stalk.
Spiderwebs balloon with bubbles of dew
while their mistresses stopple their breathing-tubes,
travelling upward and down,
inching and testing.

As soon as the sun has ripened
after noon toward the hammered gold
of sunset, it departs for its nightly reception
in the West, leaving the sky all pearls.
Mice and moles, peepers and woodcock,
speak up in twittering singsongs.
Robins yodel. Owls and night-herons
scream and crawk.

Out of sight of the sun the plants
lie quiet. They snuff their inner candles
as the moon combs through fledgling trees
to ruffle the landscape and frost their leaves
with the filigree of moonshine.
This is the time for sleep.
We will feed even better tomorrow, and after
the sun mounts high, breed till our brains burst
with the bluebell music of flickers and grackles.

Lovers by Sea-Light

the seasons pass by
sunrise noonfall moonset
two lie entwined
tides lap and hiss
at the lips of these bodies
the salt pools
gush overflow or
suck themselves dry
we lie together
as close as shore and sea

Valentines

The shining door down the hall
opens to admit to these corridors
the familiar monsters of my dreams.
They are branches that flower in winter,
pools that can never freeze
for they have swallowed arrows,
live hearts scissored from paper.
They carry my warmth to headstones
but suck my breath, just as
overcoats smother bodies.

Call Sign Aquarius

The water I am made of,
free-standing, unencumbered,
has learned to pronounce me and
call me watercourse. Call me:

a hunched and encroaching darkness
ozone clogging the nostrils
a blinding pounce of light
a chuckle of distant thunder
a clod sucking the spatter
and satisfaction of the storm
a pasture glazed with dandelions
and lupines
a bare shouldered sun
in a brisk and clarified sky
songs of a thrush spiralling up
to carol darkness into the drenched woods

In the silence of this white-plastered room,
alone and dry, deranged,
I hum like a transistor with the codes
of faraway weather.

Motley

Hairband, homespun, opera-hat, afghan,
turtle-neck, sheepskin, catskin, buckskin,
denim, dimity, beadwork, braidwork,
rags ripped off from old six-reelers—

all serve as signals to allies and enemies
that Whatintheworld may be taking the air.
Could he be banker, butcher, broker,
madman, marauder, masquerader?

Men who wear ascots, waistcoats, cheviots
are ostracized: doctors, lawyers, palaverers,
rich men and thieves (uncurious costumes).
Young men, beggar men, brawny men saunter

in pigskin, lambskin, desert boots, sandalslippers,
hairshirts and hiphuggers. Others lay footbones
bare to the broken glass, dogshit, chewing gum,
sleep in the park with guitar cases, rucksacks,
stretched on the sidewalk, curbside, fenderwise.

Whether they're indoors, outstretched, uptight,
grant them their groin bulges, hairlines, hiplines,
toenails, kneecaps, beardstubble, sticknipples,
grant them their armpits, cockpits, spitballs,
precious possessions, all body-portable.

Better go jackanapes, dogsbody, bareass
than strut through Necropolis unrecognizable,
sexless, seducible, deeply disguisable.

The Dance of the Hours
or, It's a Living

Each hour of workaday fits just as well
as my old tweed jacket which has taken years
to learn to sag its shoulders. Sixty thousand
hours have rubbed up this telephone, tattooed
the roller of the typewriter. O shelves
and drawers, what purple uprisings you've stacked
into submission! For you I've herded papers
in and out to be disposed of elsewhere—
say in the crypt, say in the dead file.
I cling to my perch between the two baskets,
what a responsible spot. I'm here to keep
things that come In from getting Out too soon.
No one will liberate those memoranda
ranked up behind their fellows in the file
unless it be the moth that flickers, remembering
the odor of our bargain. We've forged a set
of deeds, wills, seasons, my hours and I.
We grow together in one tree, sparing and spending.
We never speak of what has passed between us.
We stare at one another through a window
and wonder which will be the first to tell.

Bed Time

Few beds are stonier than one shared by a sleeper
and a waker who stares into the dark
listening to the house breathe. Children
sigh, dogs snore, clocks tick, radiators mutter.
Love past, he lies vacant. Bed carries him
to countries that his body will never visit,
regions where his mind cannot drink the water.

Feet up. Blood trickles through his head
to pass between Horn Gate and Ivory Gate.
Sleep pilot, dreamer, flying Dutchman,
he steers his ticktock course between chills and fever
bound out of Birthport for Lovepool and Death Haven.

Love past! Clandestine beds in borrowed apartments.
Fern beds, pine needles, beds for *porcheria*.
Beds whose springs have crumpled from exuberance
or rattled with anger. Beds whose backs have bent
from nightly throes of union and reunion.
'Oh bed, where first I loosed my virgin girdle . . .'
She fell upon her knees and kissed the bed.

As in a hospital where he awaits in bed
the next day's condescension of doctors,
he bleeds broken promises. Is it sailing time
for the ship of fools, the ship of the dead?
Pain lightning flickers and spatters
the four-cornered flatland of his life,
but what else is there to fall back on?
In bed we depend on nothing but bed.

Walking on Water

Sand boils up around me.
I am stung and scalded
by a war of ripples.
Barnacle skeletons
gouge at my skin.
Currents have wrestled me
for the trophy of myself
and won.
I roll in the turbid
waters at the edge
where my ankle-bones
clack together.

A few breaths ago
I paddled out bravely
and stood up alien. I crouched
in the power of my blood.
I coasted down the glacial
slope of a wave
and balanced for a heartbeat over
the quicksand surface
of the silent world.

Walking the Boundaries:
East by the Cliff

The pasture, freckled with patches
of elderly snow, flutters pale flags
of martyred goldenrod. Ice pokes and clutches
into the female cleft of the Indian rock.
From high vantage in our eldest hickory
jays engage in an antiphony
of creditable outrage
against their rivals the crows
who station themselves in the maples.

My breath is glue in my nostrils.
Mere air holds the sleeping marsh
solidly in chains, it crumples
the recent thaw's ruts
into hogback ridges
that the sun when it waxes
will take much trouble
to melt down again
into March mud.

Barren as an unlocated satellite,
this moment is dustless and rigid.
Only the gurgle and scurry
of blood-salt tides can
irrigate these badlands,

scatter the ice-floes, patiently flush
the mud-bottomed creeks, never mind remorse,
into the patiently receptive sea.

The barking of bored dogs
rattles the hard hillside.
The jays protest, chickadees chatter,
fierce finches whimper.
Pent and braggart geese
in my neighbor's corral
cackle echoes against
my iced-over windowpanes.

Our beechwoods have given up
their ghosts to mushrooms.
Plumes from grosgrain chimneys
remind me with woodsmoke
how, crisply thrusting and stretching,
roots and bowed branches conveyed
quick currents of sap
through the longtime noontimes
of longago summers.

A pewter-coloured sky
tightens up into zinc
as the momentary day flickers
toward sundown. Breath from the South
drops heathery hints of a promise,
but the North rides back in its tracks
at the near edge of dark to retract it.

This is the season of waiting for light,
of electric nights, of unrecognized footprints.
Wan woodpiles and slumbering straw
nurse reliquaries of calories
against the scorch of wind and the hiss of snow.
They sing lullabies across the chasm
between this dangerous land
and the whispering sun.

Dark Houses

For Edward Davison (1970–1898)

> *I shall come back at last,*
> *In this dark house to die.*
>> Edward Davison, 1919

I At Seventy-One. New York.

Words have finally failed this balloon of a body,
White as a side of bacon, cold as the plank
It heightens like foothills under a sheet in the morgue.
Inside it, living, smoldered poetry
Like January wasps that stir in summer houses.
Parched past a trickle now, his will had wrestled
Headlong through the pastures of his youth
In floods of love. He squandered it, spent it on girls
Who took his rings and sold them for a ribbon,
Leaving him petulance and loyalty
As stones in drought, no longer bathed by love.
In spite of years and years of wearing down,
The words whose slave he was could still surprise him.
Lying half-blind, his lips alive with poems,
In his delirium his voice cried out again
With 'Elsie Marley', 'The Tyger', 'O Mistress Mine',
'Led by a blind and teachit by a bairn'.
From the first breath in Glasgow to the last
Shudder in Mount Sinai Hospital,
Words, and the songs of words, convinced his life.
No words go walking in a darkened house.

II At Fifty. Pennsylvania.

His days of life grew drier with the years
Or dwindled into place-names on a map.
In his own eyes, what cracks across the glass,
Betrayals he had given and received?
Lord, I am not worthy to sit at Thy table.
He downed each whisky like a punishment
To keep his heart from thumping with the shame

Of memory and waste. 'The parable of the talents
Lies on my conscience like a heavy weight.'
Buried was the hate of his treacherous father
In old men whom he loved. He worked to win,
And won, their praise, as heavy as a father's,
But praise from such could never quite be trusted.
Buried, buried were all his loves and flowers
In the woman who never calmed him but inflamed
His anger. O buried deep inside inside
But bursting out in coughs that stretched and tore
His chest and neck in the tempest of his rage,
Dry places racked him with a daily taste
Of all that wrestles poetry to earth.

III   At Forty. Colorado.

Hard by these mountains, cottonwoods and creeks,
He pitched his camp, the woman at his side,
And basked in the dry light of his latest father—
President, chief scholar, neighbor, friend.
The world of London letters grew more faint,
But students clustered round. His voice, reciting,
Drew them to poetry as to a mass.
What he saw kindled in their faces helped
Him hope for recompense from poetry,
For poetry is what he spent for them.
She would not wind her arms around his arms
Nor would he cleave to her, forsaking others.
Exiled, admired, content and yet dismayed,
He came into his own as son and father
Just as he, knowingly, went down as poet.
Without the nourishment of loneliness
Or lovers to betray him, poetry
Turned from his bed, his page, but not his life.
Desertion is not charged in this affair.

IV   At Thirty. On Tour.

His heart's love now laid bare, he gives pursuit
Across an ocean, putting her to proof.

She flies before him, hesitates, surrenders,
But only for the moment. He must set
His mark on her, let her not disappear,
For she will never answer all his letters.
Sinking his past behind him, he embarks
On the Britannic Sea and lands, surprised,
At Montreal to garner his reward.
In wilderness, beside the Rangeley Lakes,
Amid the barbershops and alien corn,
He finds her. Is it he she's waiting for?
Her eyes more than her voice confess she's true.
Scanning a whole new continent for the prize
He values most, the treasure that eludes him,
He searches eagerly as ever for
The faithful woman, the approving elder,
And finds his heart's desire, as we all do:
A wife, a chief; a mother and a father.
Prizes are given him, but he must strive
To test them countless times for certainty,
For assay. Can it be true? Can it be true?
Poems have promised him it would be true.

V   At Twenty-Two. Cambridge.
His Cambridge was the Cambridge of the poets—
Dawn on the river, fervency of friendship,
Young men striving. (Dream no more of dark houses.)
His editor and benefactor, Squire,
Cool as a father in his patronage,
Lent almost every pound he could afford
Whenever he remembered to enclose it.
Spurred on, the student edited, disputed,
Wrangled and charmed. ('Breakfast with Sidney Webb.'
'Sassoon and Arnold Bennett came to tea.')
He drenched himself in poetry that held
To English tunes. His poems sprang to paper
And into print. He grieved and swore and counted
The ways his love betrayed him, while his friends,
Ackerley, Kitto, Priestley, Campbell, Kendon,

Bound by the lavish loyalties of youth,
Stood by his midnights, heard out his laments,
Read him their poems in return for his.
He was, it was said, the perfect Cambridge poet.
No one at Cambridge carried so much poetry
Close to the surface, fresh and potable.
Sluicing and plunging through a hundred months
Of loves and labors, quarrels, debts and rages,
He squandered all the energy (he mourned
In later years) that should have served to carry
His poems out of luck and into truth.
After so ravening an orgy, fear
Of weariness would trouble him forever.

VI   At Sixteen. South Shields.
His mother sits alone in the narrow house
On a Tyneside street, waiting for the weekly
Cheque to arrive from the man the children knew
As Uncle Ted. The weeks it did not come
The milkman and the grocer gave her credit
Because she always spoke to them like a lady.
When did the boy first hear the sound of poems?
Not in the slums, the collieries and streets
Where draymen, coalmen, dustmen clumped and ranted.
Not in the South Shields Empire Theatre where jugglers,
Comics and pratfall people woke the dead
At ten performances a week while he
Sat in the darkness of the street outside,
A ticket-seller at fifteen. The following year,
(Six inches yet to grow till he was grown)
He called himself eighteen and sought his fortune,
A place in Churchill's Royal Naval Division,
And set to work on his self-education.
He sat in uniform and did the duty
For five years keeping records at the Crystal Palace.
Poetry came to him, beginning with Sophocles,
Tennyson (Everyman Library), Spenser, Shakespeare,
Lamb and Coleridge. Behind them all lay

The Church of England, where still the language of Cranmer
Rang like a bell. Lord, I am not worthy to sit at Thy table.
And, seasoning this, 'Woman, her power and charm'.

VII His Rest, 1970. Massachusetts.
Now life has blunted the edges of his fury.
Mistrals of laceration and self-betrayal
Wither his bloom, bring frost to the harvest of youth.
His childhood, trodden beneath an implacable boot,
Lies motionless as memory in water
Where bones lie scattered shellmeal on the bottom.
Stricken by years of labor and rancor, all
For little but a blessing by the fathers,
The poet dies. A creature dies with him
Who had long lost the way into his poems.
We never understood his shrieks of rage
Damning the multitude of mousy deaths
That, year by year, would parch him into silence—
A swollen body lying on a plank.
Surviving him, we carry the poet's flesh
Reduced to ashes in a canister
Along a path to the summit of a cliff
Where Indians held their summer vigil
Over the shellfish marshes and the sea.
We let the bones and ashes tumble out,
Dusting the granite in their heavy fall
Until they catch and rest in crevices
Or sink dissolving in the tepid brack
Of marsh below. And now his thirsty body
Is part of the land at last, land of his children,
Where the gray ungiving stone can always stand
For fathers, thrusting up above the fields
Not ever his own, though dearer than the land
That gave him birth but never knew his name.

Ground

This stuff is what we are born from. Before my eyes
and between my fingers—grainy, sticky, chalky—
the provisions lie at hand for life to burst out of.
How stubbornly it behaves, baked hard as biscuits
in summer, yet, thawed by spring, spreading wide
to swallow a hundred horses, and in winter
rigid enough to scrape knuckles and crack bones.
It would seem to yield no passage, except that roots
as delicate as hairs can pierce hardscrabble
without a bruise or blister and hold their course
whether opposed by gravel or mud. By tasting it
farmers can guess at what may come of its favors,
whether their crops will require manure or limestone.
We savor in the first-plucked leaf of lettuce
the lingering fragrance of Sun, which slips away
with the soil that bestowed it almost within the hour,
just as fish lose their colors out of water . . .
as I would despair if you were dead.

Standing Fast:
Fox into Hedgehog

After these years of sniffing the air at hedges,
leaping so gingerly as to leave no footprints,
tiptoeing through streams to wash off my own scent,
and walking welcome at night into the houses of hens,
my paws grow clumsy; my spine curls into a hoop;
these claws must be given over to scrabbling and scuttling.

No more prancing. My snout, the air-taster,
now stiffens itself for rooting. The silken ears,
the blazing tail, the shimmering pelt, gather up
the color of gray earth. No more flight or pursuit.

Quarry for all comers, I crouch in furrows,
keep away from the light, bristle at a footfall,
my body set up for surprise. Stand fast, here, now.
No call to run quick. I know what I know.

Walking the Boundaries:
North by the Creek

Inside my human walls I sit surrounded
by scurrying music. Voices sing *Kyrie*.
My eyesight ranges out across the field.
Those acres tolerate us as their maker does,
suffering denials without a sound,
courtesies and rain without a smile.
They hover at the edge of land and sea.
Downstream, northerly, the restless waters
search up the creek twice every day
and twice a day back off to leave it dry.
At certain tides the place has the look of an island;
at others, a desert of cold mud. Crops germinate
to feed the appetites of muskrat and mackerel.
This is saltmarsh country, two-way country,
no-man's-land for gill beasts and lung beasts.
Its frontiers meander, liquefied, unmeasured.

Color fades out of the field as though the sun
had dipped into the earth to stain the clouds.
Indoors the singers climb the scale from mercy
to glory, from belief past blessing to
a resolution—the unimaginable plea
that a Lamb should grant us peace—and then are silent.
Over the land and sea, air cools and hardens.
A thrush sings its Goodnight. Among the maples
of the swamp, peepers fiddle their shrill chorus,
toads who have somewhere learned to sing like birds.
Here, where coastline edges off the forest
and the woodland's freshet leavings leak away

to modify the high tide's appetite,
I hear the woodcock's opening declaration
that he too is ready to sing. There's light enough
left for me to see the dumpy body
as it shuffles among the tufts of last year's grass,
restless and ready for nightflight. Hear the blare
of his tiny trumpet, so sharp a sound that he
must hunch his shoulders to squeeze it out. Again
and again his music sends the lively word
to the edge of the woods and out across the marsh
as though this Orpheus required his voice
to travel back and forth between the worlds
just as his wondrous delicate bill must probe
the soggy earth for worms.

                    Now we have arrived
at the edge of darkness, and the woodcock, darkened,
leaps aloft with a whir of wings. Wings?
No, music—his voice, he is singing! He rises up
past the dark treetops to the graying sky.
As he leaves the earth his song ascends
higher and higher, pitch upon pitch, spiral
after spiral. At last, at the top of his helix
three hundred feet or more, it is enough,
he can rise no farther on the updraft of this song,
he has reached a boundary. He starts to fall.
He topples from the peak, repulsed by sky.
He dips zigzag then loops and twitters earthward,
his song hot on the wingbeats of his flight
coiling in chirrups of retreating tailspin.
Plunge and flutter. Silence. He glides
from the edge of light across the edge of dark
to alight upon the very shadowed patch
of earth from which the night had lifted him.
A pause for breath. He trumpets out a warning
that this was *not* a failure. He collects
himself to ascend again, to reach beyond
the edge of the habitable world, beyond
his limits of heaviness and incarnation.

Gills dried up long since, useless on land.
Fins flowered into three-toed featherweight
tuckaway talons for pouncing and perching.
The brain, too massive to fly very far with,
dwindled in birds once flippers became wings
and danger need no longer be outwitted.
How much is left behind at boundaries!
Arising from the sea we lost our lightness.
Thought took us to the woods, where vision blurred,
for sight and mind do not take wing together.
Body at least is bound within a landscape,
an earth that holds us fastened to the seasons
for food and footing, birth and burial.
Regardless of the gifts we've left behind
and all the boundaries we cannot cross,
some power lets us press beyond our powers:
echoes of wind, of ebb and flow, of heartbeat,
singing that trickles landward with the waters,
music that clambers skyward through the dark.